101 Ways To Be A Long-Distance Super Dad ...or Mom, Too!

George Newman

R&E Publishers
2132 O'Toole Avenue
San Jose, CA 95131
Tel: (408) 432-3443
Fax: (408) 432-9221

2nd Revised Edition

Cover and interior design by Robin Collet
Illustrations courtesy of Corel Corporation, Double Exposure,
Image Club Graphics, Inc., 3G Graphics, Inc., and Robin Collet

Library of Congress Card Catalog Number 96-67465
ISBN 1-56875-188-5

To Rick, my son, who inspired this book.

Contents

Author's Note

This book is for parents who—for any reason—find themselves in one place and their children in another. While divorce can geographically separate a mom or a dad from a child, so can military service or a job requiring travel.

Parents not living under the same roof as their kids need all the help they can get to build and maintain good, strong relationships with their children.

Fifteen years ago, when I was encouraged to write the original "101 Ways to be a Long-Distance Super-Dad," the book was purchased mostly by divorced fathers. Nowadays, there is an increasing population of non-custodial mothers. I have been invited to speak at national conferences of non-custodial mothers and quickly learned that their problems and frustrations are often identical to those of non-custodial fathers.

The traditional family unit is an endangered species. Times are changing. Parenting skills must change, too. Meanwhile, religious and other organizations dedicated to preserving family values are addressing the problem and are working to keep parent and child in touch with each other regardless of how many miles or states separate them.

Long-distance parents will find ideas and suggestions offered from my original book as well as many exciting new ideas made possible by recent advances in technology. Use the ideas that work for you and your child whether it's a postcard or an e-mail message.

My best advice, whether you've been a long-distance parent for a week or ten years, is *do something*! Your child will be glad—and so will you.

1

Working Together

Do seek to cooperate with your former spouse in establishing a program for communicating as well as visiting with your children.

In most instances, mothers who have custody will encourage their children to maintain a meaningful relationship with their fathers, and vice versa. Ordinarily, a custodial parent recognizes the importance of such contact and views it as necessary for the well-rounded development of the child. It is the exception, rather than the rule, that a parent having custody will attempt to discourage a relationship between the child and non-custodial parent.

Consider the emotional stability and welfare of your child when confronted with making choices or decisions that are not directed toward cooperation. You might briefly see yourself as the winner, but your child will be the ultimate loser.

2

'Phone-Visit' Scheduling

Do try to arrange in advance the times when you will be telephoning your children. If they are quite young, this must be handled in cooperation with the custodial parent. If the children are old enough, you can make the arrangements directly with them, with the understanding, however, that they seek the approval of the custodial parent. Weekday telephoning can often pose problems for a custodial parent because of school, work schedules, transportation and the like. Also, long-distance phone rates are usually more expensive weekdays.

Most parents choose weekends to phone their kids, since long-distance rates are cheapest on Saturday and on Sunday until 5 p.m. If possible, call from a phone where you can dial directly, since using operator assistance adds significantly to the cost.

When calling your youngster, it's a good idea to ask whether dinner is about to be served or if there is any reason why 'now' isn't a good time to talk. It's an easy matter to agree to phone back in a half-hour or so, if that's more convenient.

3

Buying Kids

Don't try to buy your child. Offering or sending extravagant gifts can only prove counterproductive. And it necessarily places the custodial parent on the defensive, which isn't good for anyone. Give to your child of yourself. Give your child your time and attention. It's better for your child if you remember him or her by sending smaller gifts or token items often rather than buying an expensive gift occasionally.

There is no difference in being a non-custodial parent and remembering your child only periodically than it is to be married, living at home and lavishing your child with money-bought items rather than with your own interest, time and attention. Both will result in poor parent-child relationships.

Remember, part of being a good parent requires giving of yourself—sometimes, a lot. A checkbook simply won't do the job.

Goes Without Saying

Divorced parents will often try to get at each other through their kids. One way is by dropping critical or insulting remarks about their ex-spouse. Nothing is more harmful, both for the children and the parents. Such remarks usually result in resentment, if not retaliation. Consequently, pressure and strain are forced upon the non-custodial parent's relationship with the children. Unfortunately, such instances are not rare, mainly because emotions often run high during and after divorce. But what the parents sometimes don't realize is that everybody loses when namecalling begins.

If you have a problem, either handle it directly with your ex-spouse or through a lawyer. Leave the kids out of it altogether. If you don't have anything good to say about your ex-spouse while talking with your child, then it's far better to say nothing at all.

5

When Common Sense Lacks

There will be those times when one or the other parent gets their ire up to where phone 'visits' are made impossible. Such instances are rare, but they do happen, and the rebuffed parent is usually so angered that he or she is ready to let words fly. That is precisely the time to say nothing at all. If there's been a misunderstanding, a letter will serve to clear it up. Draft a letter to the ex-spouse, but don't mail it. Reread and edit it the next day. Then, let a friend look at it and make further suggestions. Once that's been done, rewrite and mail it. If the reply is reasonable, then common sense has scored a victory.

If the custodial parent refuses to allow you further phone 'visits' with your kids, or if there is no reply, then secure the services of a lawyer. Don't try to handle it yourself—you'll make a mess. When you hire a lawyer, make sure he or she specializes in domestic law. Make inquiries, acquaint yourself with those attorneys available and understand that you pay no more for the best lawyer than you do for a mediocre one. Ask about fees, length of time needed and the prospects for reaching your objective. It cannot be overstated how important it is that you hire a capable attorney who specializes in *domestic law*, rather than a general-practice lawyer.

Always let your lawyer represent you, and don't make a move—especially in contacting your ex-spouse—without first checking with your lawyer.

6

Forgetting's Easy

Whether you phone your children once a week or more or less often, you'll find it's easy to forget certain things you wanted to talk about.

A solution is to keep within reach a running list of such items, either on a scrap of paper in your pocket or possibly on your home desk calendar on a page marked with the date that you next intend to phone. By doing this, you'll find it's amazing how much more meaningful the conversations will be. There won't be as many gaps, oh's and ah's, and wondering just what you can talk about to fill the time. Also, be sure to write down questions that you want to ask your kids, such as what they have been learning in school, places they've visited, movies they've seen or new friends they might have made. Once you've gotten into the habit of using the list, scarcely a day will pass when you don't add a notation of some sort.

Remember, your list of things to talk about is the backbone of a long-distance phone relationship. Use the list often to make the most of it. And, when your children are old enough, encourage them to do the same.

7

Touch of Class

Whether your child is old enough to read or whether your letters are read aloud by your ex-spouse, you'll find that appearance can be almost as important as content.

Choose a distinctive, though not necessarily expensive, type of stationery—one which will be easily identified by your child when the mail arrives. If possible, try to stay with one particular type for a period of time, such as a solid-color sheet and envelope. Though often hard to find (one father reported visiting six stationery shops until he found them), solid-color envelopes stand out clearly in a stack of mail. Your child will spot it immediately and holler, "Here's a letter from Daddy (or Mommy)!" Another plus is the element of continuity, which, for a child of divorced parents, is especially important.

Stationery that contains sketches, photos or certain theme designs is also attractive to youngsters. Boys often like sports or aviation themes, while girls enjoy themes with dolls, flowers or horses. My own choice for the best selection goes to the father who always wrote on brownbag-type paper and envelope, using either a blue felt-tip pen or blue typewriter ribbon. His letters always stood out.

Different Postage Stamps

A small but interesting part of your letters to your children are the postage stamps you affix on the envelope.

Who notices such things, you ask? When the U.S. Postal Service issued a commemorative set containing the flags of all 50 states, I bought a sheet. Each week, when I sent my son a letter, I pasted the flag of a different state on the envelope. At the end of a year, my son proudly announced that he had collected the entire set from the letters I had sent him.

Whether a youngster is a stamp collector or not, there is much about history, geography, the arts and sciences to be gleaned from our nation's stamps. Next time, instead of buying the usual booklet or coil of stamps, ask at the post office whether there are any commemorative stamps available. Ordinarily there is a new issue every couple of weeks. Try it.

Stuck on Stickers

Pasting stickers on your correspondence to your children can enhance an already interesting and attractive letter. Walk into any variety store, stationery shop or discount drug store and choose from a wide selection of stickers. An attractive location to paste stickers is on the back of the envelope, just where the V-flap adheres to the envelope. Nowadays, you'll find stickers of all types, shapes and sizes. Choose the stickers that best relate to your son's or daughter's interests or hobbies. You'll be surprised what a difference such a small thing makes. And, besides, kids love them.

10

Save Those Clippings

How often do you come across something in a newspaper or magazine that you know would interest your child?

It might be a sports-page article or perhaps a tongue twister, quiz item or even a joke. It takes only seconds to clip it out and lay it aside until you are ready to send your next letter or fax. Also, be sure to mention it when you talk next on the phone; it could well become a topic of conversation. And don't hesitate to ask questions on the subjects. Seek your child's reactions and opinions. Use the clippings to evoke discussion. And always keep on the lookout for animal photos. Younger children, especially, enjoy animals; and most daily newspapers seldom allow a week to pass by without publishing at least one unusual or interesting animal photo.

Remember, too, that coin-operated photocopy machines are available almost everywhere—in case you find something you'd like to send, but the article cannot be clipped out.

11

How Do You Spell . . .?

One of the most spellbinding games (pardon the pun) that you can play with your child via phone involves spelling words.

We'll assume that your child is at an age where he or she is learning to spell and could enjoy the challenge of the game. During each phone call, quiz your child on perhaps three or four spelling words, selected in advance, and of course, geared to their learning level. You might choose to make one of the selected words slightly more difficult than the others, simply to keep interest in the game. At the same time, invite your child to search for the three or four most difficult words he or she can find during the next week or so, and have him or her ready to challenge you the next time you phone. My son and I became so wrapped up in this game that we began keeping each other's 'batting average' or percentage of words spelled correctly.

If you haven't considered it, just think for a moment about the amount of time your child spends looking up spelling words to challenge you. Such a learning experience can often be as productive, or more so, than a classroom spelling lesson.

12

What's the Capital of . . .?

Asking your child to identify U.S. and foreign capitals can be a rewarding experience as well as providing a format for a fun game. The reward comes because it is rare that a child is afforded an opportunity to put to work what he or she has learned in a geography class, for example. So when you ask your child for the capital of Delaware or Switzerland or Australia, he or she will often be delighted to show you how much they have learned. As in many other telephone games, it is important to also allow your child to challenge you with similar questions, as it goes both ways.

13

From George Washington to . . .

Youngsters seem to find a challenge in memorizing the names and order of ascendancy of U.S. presidents. It's much like knowing all the models of cars or names of screen stars. However, there seems to be something special about presidents. If your child has already been exposed to the list, either through the classroom or otherwise, try asking one or two each time you phone. And you might start with the easy ones and work up to the harder ones.

14

Cards for Holidays

Events like birthdays and Christmas require special attention on your part. However, it's the less-important holidays and other occasions that are so often overlooked when simply sending a card would tell your child that you remembered. When your children are very young, it's especially important to keep them in mind before the arrivals of Halloween, Easter, Thanksgiving, Valentine's Day and other special days, including graduation, departure on a trip and the like.

Appropriate greeting cards can be purchased at most stationery and variety stores, and neighborhood drug stores at minimal cost. It's another way of letting them know that you care. It's also a nice idea to occasionally insert a treat into the card envelope. This could perhaps include a few gift coupons for McDonald's (these are usually accepted nationwide), Baskin-Robbins ice-cream chain or any other coupon or gift certificate issued by a national chain operation. And there's no need to overdo. It's the thought that's important.

15

Choosing Those Gifts

One of the most common questions asked by long-distance parents is, "What can I buy them?" The problem is not as difficult as it may at first seem.

When birthdays, Christmas and other special occasions approach, the natural tendency is to panic and then reach for the checkbook. But neither is really necessary. Sending money is a last resort, and should be reserved only for that purpose. A good move is to inquire several weeks ahead, when talking with your child via phone, as to what he or she might like as a birthday or Christmas present. Keep in mind that holiday mail is heavy and moves slowly, so allow plenty of time. It's also a good idea to talk with friends who have children and learn what some of the current popular gift items are. Then, when you talk with your own child, you will have a starting point. If you are divorced and on reasonably amicable terms with your ex-spouse, he or she might also make some suggestions.

Although you can often save by purchasing your gifts at a discount store, there is also a disadvantage. Most discount stores will not mail gift items for you, and if you ship them yourself and they arrive damaged, you must hassle with the Postal Service for compensation. Though the price might be slightly higher, most major department stores will cheerfully package and mail your gift for you, at the same time assuming full responsibility for its arrival in good condition.

16

Magazine Subscriptions

A frequent and steady reminder to youngsters that their long-distance parent remembers them is a subscription to a magazine of their choice. The field is wide and varied, but specialized enough for you to find just the right magazine that will complement your son's or daughter's interests or hobbies. A visit to the children's section of your local library offers an excellent means of getting acquainted with the complete list of publications. There you may inspect them first-hand and also speak with the librarian. He or she can assist you in preparing a list of possible choices, which you can later discuss with your child. If your child is beyond the age of interest in juvenile publications, consider subscriptions to sports and outdoor magazines, auto, computer, aviation, hobby publications and horse magazines, often the favorite of girls.

17

Gift Memberships

Does your child's community have a science museum, planetarium society or film-making club? If so, many such organizations offer weekend programs specially designed for youngsters. You can inquire via mail or phone about the organization and its special programs, and receive a brochure detailing information. Nothing might excite your son or daughter more than a year's membership in the junior division of one of these groups. Many sponsoring organizations schedule special classes, field trips and often furnish transportation for the kids.

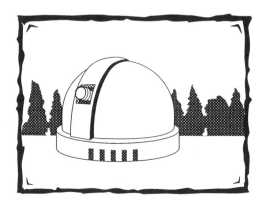

18

TV Offers

Quite often, as you watch TV, there are opportunities to discover an advertised offer that your child would enjoy. Some examples include membership in TV fan clubs, copies of various promotional coloring books, brochures, official cups and drinking glasses and chances to enter the child's name in various contests. Also, several national food and confection chains frequently advertise memberships in birthday clubs. Send them your child's name, and the youngster will receive a birthday coupon worth a free dinner, admission to an event or merchandise. It's just another way of letting your child know that he or she is on your mind.

19

Like Magic

All youngsters like magic tricks. And, even more, they thrill at any opportunity to perform magic themselves.

Ordinarily, packaged magic tricks sold at retail are not easy to find. Since most department stores and variety stores don't often include them among their regular merchandise, it's necessary to consult the yellow pages for a specialty shop.

In many directories, you'll find these stores listed under the headings, 'Magic Supplies' or, 'Magician's Supplies.' Usually available are a large number of inexpensive magic tricks. Of course, there are some rather expensive as well as elaborate varieties, also. However, if you explain to the salesperson what you intend to do with your purchase, and give the age of your child, you'll find most to be very helpful. Be sure to ask the salesperson to demonstrate the trick before you buy it, so that you can discuss it with your youngster.

After your child has received the trick, encourage him or her to attempt to read the instructions and learn how to perform the trick without your

assistance. However, if your child should encounter difficulty or seek your assistance, then you will be in a good position to help.

If the youngster offers you positive feedback, consider sending a new trick each month or so, or even a book on magic tricks. Many youngsters who become accomplished at performing magic often hire themselves out to stage magic shows at birthday parties and special events. It's good, healthy fun, costs little, and builds self-confidence.

20

Watching TV "Together"

The strongest relationships established between individuals often are keyed to common interests. Those between parent and child are no exception. In this context, you'll find that youngsters are frequently willing, if not eager, to discuss with adults certain television programs they watch. While getting a youngster to detail information about themselves or their activities can prove frustrating, it's not the case when it comes to TV. Find out your child's favorite programs and begin watching those that you can.

Parents who are concerned about the quality of some network shows should be aware that the nation's non-commercial public broadcasting stations offer a wide range of quality programs, many of which are suitable for children. Also, the commercial networks periodically present programs specially produced for family viewing. Since many of these specials are promoted well in advance, you have an opportunity to inform your child about the show. Then, you will both have an opportunity to watch it "together" and discuss it afterward.

21

Wish You Were Here

Do you like to receive postcards? Youngsters do, too. Whenever you depart your hometown, there's an opportunity to send your child an interesting picture postcard. Even if your trip involves a drive of only 20 miles, there's the novelty of receiving an out-of-town postcard. The best locations to find such postcards are drugstores and variety stores. If you are at an airport, there's almost always a newsstand or souvenir shop offering a wide selection of such cards.

Because finding a place to purchase postage stamps is often a problem, here's a tip: Buy a dozen stamps appropriate for affixing to postcards the next time you're at the post office. Place the stamps in your wallet. Then you'll have them available when you need quick postage. Also, there's no reason why you can't periodically send your child a picture postcard from the city where you reside. Remember, whether you are traveling on business, visiting a tourist attraction or simply shopping at a neighborhood drug or discount store—think postcards!

22

Movie Reviews

Most kids like movies, and your child can qualify as a film reviewer, with an audience of one assured—you. The next time you talk with your son or daughter via phone, ask whether they have seen any new movies or videos recently. If so, could they tell you about them?

By asking them questions, it will help them next time to remember to cover all the key elements ordinarily included in a movie review. Without appearing to be instructional, such an experience prepares a youngster for future school assignments, in which organization is a critical element. And, too, reviewing movies is fun.

On the other side of the coin, you might try reviewing some movies *you've* seen.

You and your youngster should seek to avoid the mistake too often made, and that is revealing the climax. Ever try to guess how many people decide not to see a film because they've been told the ending? Don't number yourself among them.

23

Sending School Work Samples

Do you remember when you were a kid how proud you were to carry home your first crayon-colored picture? Since you can't be in the household when your child brings home his or her completed work from school, there is a backup means for getting a look at it. It's called the U.S. Postal Service, and the material can be delivered to your mailbox within a few days. If there's a fax available, better yet.

Send large, stamped, pre-addressed manila mailing envelopes (size 10 x 13 inches are best). Once you've received the schoolwork—whether it be a colored picture, an essay, term paper or project—be sure to offer your youngster lots of feedback. Try to be laudatory and positive whenever you can. Ask lots of questions. Let your child know, unmistakably, that you are interested. Also, there's no reason why a continued steady flow of these papers, etc., can't be maintained through and including high-school age.

There is no substitute for a parent who cares, no matter how great the mileage distance between parent and child.

24

News Events

Is your youngster reaching junior-high-school age? How well informed is he or she about the important news of the world?

From time to time, results of various studies or spot surveys are published showing the American people to be among the most poorly informed in the world. For example, it is not uncommon to find that upwards of one-third of all U.S. adults interviewed in such a survey cannot correctly cite the name of the vice president of the United States. Only a fraction can provide the name of the secretary of state, and a few are able to name perhaps one of the senators from their home state.

You can help to remedy this, at least as concerns your child, by attempting to discuss with him or her some of the week's major events, when talking via phone. Also, determine whether your child watches the evening news on network TV, and if the household subscribes to a daily newspaper. The importance of having access to a daily paper—even if it isn't read each day—cannot be overemphasized. As it turns out, the middle- and upper-income classes predominantly are among newspaper subscribers while those in the lower socio-economic classes are not. It is

suggested that there exists a strong correspondence between those who keep informed and those who enjoy a higher standard of living.

If your child's household doesn't receive a daily paper, you might consider making a gift of such a subscription to your youngster. But, above all, keep the discussion going, ask for opinion and feedback on major world and national issues, and seize the opportunity to acknowledge your child's interests by providing a verbal pat on the back whenever he or she rises to the occasion.

25

The Hometown Newspaper

Your child's hometown newspaper can provide a valuable tool in keeping you informed of events and activities occurring within his or her environment. If your youngster lives in or within proximity of a metropolitan area, the daily newspaper from that metropolitan area will probably be available at the main library wherever you are living. Also, many libraries stock Sunday papers from large metropolitan areas.

Checking the newspaper every couple of weeks (usually, you'll find the Sunday editions most helpful) will enable you to find what's happening on the local sports and entertainment scenes, also. Should you learn that an important sports competition is scheduled, or perhaps the arrival of the circus, or a performance by a ballet road company, you might wish to ask your child whether he or she would like to attend. If so, you can arrange to make a gift of the ticket (and the ticket for the accompanying adult, if that is appropriate).

Reading the newspaper will also make it possible for you to have on hand material to discuss on those occasions during a phone talk when you both seem to run out of topics. If you can't find the newspaper you are seeking in a public library, try a college or university library. If that fails, inquire at a large news and magazine shop. As a last resort, you can write to the circulation department of the newspaper and arrange to have it mailed to you, either every Sunday or, if that's too frequent, you can order a single issue simply by sending the correct amount, plus postage.

26

The $128,000 Question

How well-developed is your youngster's knowledge of a special subject? Whether it's football, American history, national capitals or rock music, this telephone game enables you to entertain yourself and your child—while you both learn.

Patterned after the original TV program, the game uses make-believe money. Begin by asking your child to select a subject. The first question, which ordinarily should be a less difficult one, is worth $1,000. If your child correctly answers the question, the next one is worth $2,000...and on up to $128,000. If at any time your child fails to answer a question correctly (the tougher questions are often multiple-part), the game ends and you begin all over. You can reverse roles with your child, and you can select a subject and answer questions.

Some persons who play the game find it possible to ad-lib the entire game, taking and structuring questions from personal knowledge. Others might prefer to prepare in advance or take the questions from a special book, etc. Although the money figures are, of course, makebelieve, it is sometimes a greater challenge to youngsters if they know they will receive a token award if they complete the quiz through the $128,000 question. Perhaps advising your child that you will be sending a small gift could provide such an incentive.

27

Teacher Contact

Ask any schoolteacher why Johnny can't read, and you will be told that a major part of the problem lies with a lack of parental interest.

Make it a priority on your next trip to visit your child to confer with his or her teachers. Explain to the teachers that though you can't be together with your child every day, you are in regular contact. Point out that you discuss your child's homework and progress in class during your phone conversations, but that you feel such is not enough. Ask the teachers what you can do to help, beyond what you have already mentioned. You might also wish to provide the teachers with your address and phone number, and request they phone you collect whenever appropriate.

These suggestions are not only for youngsters who might be encountering difficulty in their classes. Your child might be an "A" student, and establishing closer contact with the teacher could help your child in developing his or her potential even more fully. And when you return home, remember that a note of thanks to the teacher is always appreciated.

28

Appreciation Letters

Because most kids are at some time involved in activities requiring a volunteer adult leader or instructor, it means that someone is giving of themselves on behalf of your child. Most all of these adult volunteers enjoy what they do, whether it be coaching Little League Baseball, leading Cub Scouts or Brownie Scouts, teaching Sunday school, etc. Essentially, the reward is intrinsic. However, as a distant parent who is unable to take your turn at volunteering (if such be the case), it is an invaluable gesture if you take time to express your appreciation to those volunteers who are working with your child.

One time, I was fortunate to visit my son when he played on a Little League Baseball team, and I met his volunteer coach. In addition to expressing my thanks on the spot, I also took time to write the coach a personal letter when I returned home telling him how much I appreciated the fine work he was doing for the boys on the team, and how I had observed great improvement in my son's performance as well as his enthusiasm.

No matter who it is that extends themselves for your child, a note of appreciation from you will always be welcome.

29

Souvenir Programs

Nowadays, whenever there is a major sports event on TV, such as the World Series, Super Bowl, All-Star Game, etc., special souvenir programs are usually printed. Quite often, such souvenir programs are promoted weeks in advance over the TV network telecasting the event. Viewers are furnished an address to which to send their advance orders.

Should your youngster plan to watch these events on TV, certainly nothing will enhance his or her enjoyment more than having a copy of the official souvenir program in hand when the telecast begins. And if you employ your imagination, you will find that souvenir programs for almost any sports event can also be ordered directly from the concessions department of the home team where an event is to be contested. This holds true, regardless of whether such a program is being promoted by the TV network.

All you need do is select the particular game or team in which your youngster is interested (it need not be a major event) and write, requesting cost and instructions for purchasing an official program, or perhaps a team yearbook. The team will mail it either to you or directly to your child at your request.

30

When Friends Travel

Although it might seem unimportant, here's another opportunity to remind your child that you care and are often thinking about him or her. Whenever a friend or relative takes a trip that will send them to or through the area where your child lives, ask whether he or she will have a few moments to spare.

If you are satisfied that you are not imposing, request that the person telephone your child—during reasonable hours, of course—and explain that he or she is in town for a brief duration and wants to deliver greetings from you. The person might very often find themselves only on a brief stopover, awaiting a change of planes. But a phone call takes only a few minutes. If the person indicates a wish to do so, and has available time, he or she might arrange a brief visit to your child's home and take along a gift from you. Such a visit should be scheduled in advance, with the approval of the custodial parent.

Sometimes, a friend might have children of his or her own, and will be traveling together with them. In such an instance, your child would likely be delighted to meet the other youngsters.

Remember, you are the creative director in such instances, and whatever you arrange—so long as good judgment is exercised—will be appreciated by your child.

31

Reading Poetry

The enjoyment of poetry isn't limited to adults. Often, kids are more interested in poems than their elders. Naturally, the poetry you select to read to your child via phone should be appropriate and easy to understand.

Perhaps my all-time favorite poem which I shared with my son was "Casey at the Bat." I have read the poem aloud over the phone to my son no less than a half-dozen times over the years, and it never loses its impact.

There are also poems especially suited for girls. The best way to find them is to visit the children's section of your neighborhood library and ask a librarian for assistance. If you don't want to check out a book of poems, you can always copy the poem using one of the coin-operated machines available at most libraries.

Next time you phone your child, surprise him or her with a poem they will enjoy.

32

Watching Special Events on TV

Super Bowl? World Series? Swan Lake? You can share such experiences with your youngster. Seek to determine in advance when your son or daughter will be watching a major televised event. Then, plan on telephoning—preferably on the weekends, when rates are lowest—at about the time the telecast begins. You might wish to watch the first 10 minutes or so together, then hang up and call back during half-time or intermission. After perhaps an additional 10 minutes of together-watching, break again and then phone back during the remaining 10 minutes of the event, which will often be the most climactic.

My son and I have often watched Sunday afternoon NFL football games together by phone. Sometimes, we were pulling for opposite teams, which tended to enliven the conversation. We can now recall in detail some of those games of a few years ago, and remind each other, in fun, who was supporting which team, and who won and who lost.

Total cost for such an experience should be no more than about 30 minutes' long-distance time. And if you can manage it within the low-rate period, it's a real bargain.

33

Planning Those Together Days

Because they're precious moments, you will want to carefully plan, well in advance, your periodic get-togethers with your child.

One of the best ways to do this is with your child's help. After you have established the visiting dates and firmed up your travel arrangements, etc., take a pencil and draw a calendar on an ordinary sheet of $8^1/_2$ x 11 inch paper. Leave enough space in the date squares so you can fill in whatever activities you might plan. For example, if you and your child will be spending two weeks together, draw a calendar containing 14 squares. Discuss with your youngster the best use for the time. It's not necessary, and perhaps not desirable, to fill all of the time in advance. Open days are, in fact, a good idea, as opportunities may arise at the last moment. Generally speaking, I prefer to have in hand a community entertainment calendar, sports schedules and a list of interesting places to visit within a day's drive before I phone my son, seeking his suggestions.

Also, it isn't necessary to spend a lot of money on entertainment. Your child will enjoy his or her visit with you, perhaps even more, if you select activities which focus on the outdoors. Outings to parks, playing ball, hikes, barbecues and swimming are almost always enjoyed by youngsters. Combine those with a balance of household or garden chores, and perhaps a special treat, such as tickets to a major-league ball game or live stage production.

34

Creative Recording

Do you own a tape recorder? VCR? Camcorder? If used to maximum advantage, these devices can provide you with a valuable added dimension for contact with your child.

When my son was seven years old, his favorite TV program was "The Six Million Dollar Man" which aired over one of the major networks on Sunday evenings. He would always become excited when it came time for the program, beginning with the pre-show introduction or lead-in, a 30-second piece of footage which was repeated each week, mainly for the benefit of new viewers to familiarize them with the bionic hero's background.

One Sunday evening, I taped the audio portion of "The Six Million Dollar Man" introduction. The next time my son and I visited on the phone, I surprised him by playing the intro without any advance notice. He was thrilled and enjoyed it, to say the least.

An audio tape recorder can also be used for collecting an assortment of brief conversations, messages or any special sounds or words you wish to share with your child. An example might be a simple "hello" from a

neighbor or friend which you can play back during your next phone conversation. Also, you can use the recorder to send your child a "talking letter."

Meanwhile, as technology advances and costs for audio/visual equipment become more affordable, more long-distance parents are enjoying the use of VCRs and camcorders to communicate with their children.

Creative ideas for using video equipment are unlimited. Through this medium you can share with your child narrated viewings of your home, workplace, hobbies, travel and other leisure activities. Often, this can be done in the reverse with your child sending you his or her video tapes.

35

School Photographs

Some of the best pictures of youngsters often are the inexpensive color photos taken at school by commercial photographers. Ask your child or former spouse to send you one of these photos each year, and offer to pay whatever the cost. The pictures are often available in different sizes, and extra prints can usually be ordered. The larger prints are ideal for framing. Some parents like to have a framed photo of their child on their desk at work or on the mantelpiece at home. Smaller prints can be carried in a wallet or can be displayed in a frame serially, year after year.

36

Snapshots Span Distance

Whenever possible, take snapshots of important events, and send them to your child. These may include: a trip, a gathering of friends or relatives, an excursion or outing, a move into a new home or place of business, purchase of a new car or some item of recreational equipment (a boat, a pair of skis, a motorcycle or snowmobile) or the addition of a pet. Pictures are often much more informative than words, especially for younger children, and a photo included in your letters periodically will serve to enhance their content. Get into the habit of thinking "photo," and your child will be the beneficiary.

37

Twenty Questions

A favorite game of many youngsters is "Twenty Questions," also often called "Mineral, Animal or Vegetable." The best part about the game is that it can effectively be played on the phone.

It goes without saying that when your child is young, you should make the item to be guessed as easy as appropriate—but not too easy. The type of challenges your child will enjoy most are those that require him or her to use up perhaps 15 or more of the 20 questions available. You can provide some hints if needed, so that your child doesn't feel defeated and subsequently tire of the game.

As your child develops, you will naturally want to increase the level of difficulty of the items to be guessed. Among some tough ones I have either given or received (the game works well in *both* directions, don't forget!) are: the moustache of a famous baseball player; the glasses of a president; one of the eyes of the Sphinx and the candles on a movie star's birthday cake (shown on network TV).

Finally, it's a good idea to lead off by announcing whether the object to be guessed is "general" or "specific." For example, *any* moustache would be "general," but the baseball player's moustache is a "specific" object.

38

Helping With Homework

As your child advances in school, homework assignments increase in quantity and difficulty. During your periodic phone talk with your child, ask what homework assignments he or she is doing. You will often find you have some knowledge or background of the subject, and may be of help.

Resourcefulness in such instances counts, too. An example I recall, some years ago, was when my son was assigned to prepare a report on a country of his choice as a project for a geography class. He had chosen Trinidad and Tobago, and subsequently found that there existed little information about that nation in his school library. For a starter, I suggested that he look in the encyclopedia, and then promised him that I would do what I could to get him some more material.

The next morning, I phoned the Trinidad and Tobago Tourist Office in New York City. A polite employee took my son's name and address, and assured me that a packet containing geographic and historical information would be mailed to him promptly with the compliments of the Trinidad and Tobago government.

I paid for a two-minute long-distance call and two days later, my son, living in Florida, received the packet—much to his delight—and immediately became his class expert on Trinidad and Tobago.

39

Those Little Books— and Larger Ones, Too!

You can start mailing books to your child when he or she is as young as age two. For such youngsters of early ages, to whom the book will be read aloud by a parent or other adult, the small fairy-tale or animal books are ideal. There are, of course, a wide variety. These are frequently found in a section of the supermarket where you do your grocery shopping. The books are lightweight, illustrated in color and designed to be read to young children. Most are educational and surprisingly inexpensive.

It's a good idea to browse through the books you select to ensure that they are designed for a child the age of your youngster. You'll also want to know something about the subject so that you can discuss it later via phone.

As your child grows older and begins to read independently, he or she will likely develop an interest (you can help in that direction) in some of the popular series books, such as the Hardy Boys or Nancy Drew mysteries. Or perhaps Encyclopedia Brown mysteries. To purchase these books, you will have to visit a bookstore, where they are readily available or can be ordered. You will also discover that once your child becomes involved with one of these series, he or she will seem to rapidly devour every successive installment you send.

Blessed is the child who reads. In this day, when a disturbing percentage of high-school graduates and even college students are unable to read at a satisfactory level, you can count your youngster as fortunate if an interest in books is taken early.

And, when you mail the books at the post office, don't forget to request the special book rate. It's far less expensive than regular postage.

Collecting Stamps

As distinct from an earlier chapter, in which it was suggested that different postage stamps be used on your letters, this portion is directed toward those whose youngsters are actively collecting stamps. Stamp collecting, especially worldwide stamp collecting, provides a child with a great opportunity to broaden his or her horizons while having fun. In addition to learning something about the language of each country, there is also information about its history and geography.

But that's not all. The 11-year-old son of a friend, whom I encouraged early on in his collecting, one day complained that he was unable to collect any additional Austrian stamps without purchasing them from a dealer. I suggested that he go to the public library and ask assistance in locating the names and addresses of any stamp collectors' publications in Austria. He returned with the names of two publications and wrote to each asking if they would print his name and address and mention that he was seeking Austrian pen pals who collected stamps. He received a dozen replies and to this date remains in correspondence and exchanges stamps with three or four individuals.

It's not necessary for a youngster to buy stamps, especially if he or she is collecting worldwide. You can save stamps from foreign letters for your child as well as

asking business associates and friends to do the same.
Your child can also prevail on relatives and neighbors to
save stamps. Or your child can write to U.S. embassies
and consulates abroad, most of which, as a matter of
policy, are pleased to furnish as a courtesy a few current-
issue cancelled stamps of that country. There are also
junior stamp clubs in many areas of the country,
providing a forum for youngsters to meet and exchange
stamps.

Above all, stamp-collecting teaches a youngster
resourcefulness. You can help in this regard by encouraging your child at each step of the way by offering
suggestions and asking questions.

41

Baseball Cards

That yarn told on TV commercials about trading thirty Marv Throneberry cards for one Carl Furillo is only partially a joke. Kids who are baseball fans will often go to great lengths to get their hands on that one player card they're missing.

In past years, it was often necessary to purchase packages of bubble gum to get the cards. Nowadays, they are still furnished with packages of gum, but can be purchased separately. Also, there exists a flourishing, high-priced market among collectors of cards who specialize in the 1940s and 1950s. However, for the typical youngster, there's no need to get into such expensive dealings. The current card sets will most often meet their requirements, and there are annually several hundred new cards from which to draw. Discussing with your youngster via phone which cards he is missing will enable you to occasionally provide something intensely sought by your child.

Recently, football cards have also become popular. You might want to check around and get yourself updated.

42

Ask Me a Riddle

Most kids—and adults, too—love riddles, and your neighborhood library is a good source for a wide selection of riddle books. Such books are usually shelved in the children's section of the library.

It's usually best to check out one book at a time. Take it home and read it over. If you find some riddles that are suitable for your child, place scrap-paper markers between the appropriate pages. Then use a copying machine to make copies of those riddles you wish to share with your child. This enables you to return the book within the time limit, but meanwhile allows you to keep those riddles you want—for use at a later time.

Many long-distance parents prefer to parcel the riddles out, offering one during each phone call. Youngsters frequently look forward to receiving a new riddle each time and will ask you if you forget to provide one.

43

Play Chess via Mail (or E-mail)

A tradition dating back perhaps to the establishment of the first mail service, playing chess in such fashion often provides a tantalizing challenge. The chief drawback, of course, is that completing a game can require many months.

Needed are two complete chess sets—one in your home and the other at your child's. You'll also need a book or manual detailing the rules and containing a sketch showing the numerical board positions and the letter-numerical designation of each chess piece. Once you have covered the rules with your son or daughter, and assuming that you both enjoy the game, they will be awaiting the arrival of your postcard in the mail, signaling your first move. As likely you will, too.

Of course, if you and your child both have access to a computer and the Internet, you can play via e-mail.

44

Managing Fantasy Baseball

Start your own league with friends and co-workers. Then share the managing chore with your son or daughter, via long distance. Draft baseball superstars, choose lineups and make player trades. Standings are based on daily newspaper box scores.

In brief, here's how: Bring together 8 or 10 interested friends and hold a draft meeting prior to the start of the major league season. Draw lots to determine the order of drafting, then proceed for 18 rounds until each person has chosen 18 players, all of whom are hitters, rather than pitchers. Next, a pitchers' draft of eight rounds is conducted with each person selecting eight pitchers, preferably those who start games.

Prior to opening day, and at the beginning of each week during the season, each person submits a starting lineup to the elected league secretary. The lineup includes a player for each of the eight field positions (outfielders are free-floating and are allowed to play in any field—left, center or right) plus a designated hitter. Any player may be chosen as the designated hitter. Also submitted are the names of five pitchers.

Although all of the 26 players on your team might actually be performing during a given week, only the production of those designated in your starting lineup is actually tabulated toward your point total. The others are considered reserves during that week. A starting player receives one point for each single, RBI, run scored or stolen base. A double counts two points, a triple, three; and a home run, four points. Pitchers receive one point for each inning pitched in a winning game plus a bonus of five points for a complete game shutout and 10 extra points for a no-hit game. "League" standings are posted weekly, with total points added cumulatively through the entire season.

Some fantasy leagues collect a small "franchise fee" at the start of each season and use the funds toward the purchase of trophies at the end. Sometimes, the money is used for an awards dinner.

League members can apply their own creativity to making new rules, often designed to suit their individual needs and convenience. Can you imagine talking over lineup strategy with your child each week? Also, consider the thrill of rooting for "your own player" during a televised game. During a six-month season, your child will look forward to receiving the official league standings in the mail or via fax each week. And be sure that the league secretary lists you *and* your child as co-managers. There's nothing more satisfying for your youngster than seeing his or her name in the standings each week.

45

Fantasy Football, Too!

Similar in basic design to fantasy baseball, football league participants (a group of 8 to 10 individuals or partnerships) start with a draft and rules meeting prior to the opening of the pro football season.

All players are up for grabs in the draft, and each participant is entitled to draft 15 players, including reserves. A starting lineup consists of a quarterback, two running backs, two wide receivers, a tight end and a kicker. It is advisable to draft a backup or reserve for each of the seven positions, with an extra reserve available for the position of your choice.

Although all of the players drafted might actually be playing on the field on a particular weekend, the "manager" of each fantasy team must designate which seven of his players' performances will be counted toward his credit. Those whom he designates thusly are termed "starters," while the remaining players are considered "reserves" on that weekend, though they might actually perform on the field and possibly score. The reserves' points, however, are not counted.

Counted points are determined by whether a "starting" player is involved in a scoring play. If a running back carries the ball 89 yards and is tackled on the one-yard line, for instance, he earns nothing. But if the same player runs the ball across the goal line from the one-yard line, he is credited with the score. In a passing play, both the passer and receiver are credited, although the passer might be a member of your team, and the receiver might play for one of your "league" opponents.

Separate scoring tables are established by the league for passing, receiving, running and kicking. For example, a one-yard touchdown run might be worth three league points while a run for a TD of between 11 and 20 yards might be worth four points. From 21 to 30 yards, five points, and so on. Such scoring tables are established by the league members themselves.

Lineups are submitted to the league secretary prior to the start of each weekend's play. The fantasy team receiving the highest number of points each weekend is declared the weekly winner and receives a token prize. Points are added cumulatively throughout the season, and the weekly posted standings are based on total accumulated points. The team having the most points at the end of the season is the winner.

In some leagues, members arrange to play their fellow opponents in head-to-head competition, drawing up a league schedule prior to the start of the season. In such cases, the team with the most points in each separate weekend contest is the winner of that particular game and receives credit for a game win. Standings are determined by won-and-lost records. If there is a tie at the end of the season, total accumulated points are used to break the tie.

During football season, my son and I spent considerable time on the phone discussing draft strategy and agonizing over our weekly lineups much like professional coaches or managers. We also allowed much weight to the weekly injury reports, which we studied carefully. And, of course, we both anxiously awaited the distribution of the league standings following each weekend's play. These were immediately mailed or faxed to my son.

46

Letter-Writing: Lost Art?

Encouraging your child to write a letter, you will find, is no easy matter, regardless of his or her age. Why? Because youngsters nowadays are not learning to write. We are in the electronic age where the TV and dozens of other convenient gadgets have rendered the art of writing almost obsolete. But *almost* is not *completely*, and letters must still be written at times when no alternative exists.

A few years ago, the University of California at Berkeley, which accepts applicants only from among the top 10 percent of the state's high-school graduates, reported that a majority of entering freshmen were unable to pass a writing competency test, and most were required to undergo refresher courses in basic English composition.

If you can successfully encourage, entice or otherwise positively motivate your child to write a letter at least once a month, you will have achieved a major break-through. And your child will be the richer for it, as he or she will then number among a small minority of U.S. schoolchildren who maintain such skills.

Most importantly, you must write your child often, setting an example for letter format through your own letters. Inform your youngster that you are most interested in learning what he or she has done in the last week or two—where they have gone, new friends they have met, etc. Explain that questions such as, "How are you?" don't make interesting reading. Finally, you must offer an incentive or reward for all letters received. It need not be expensive; perhaps, a "well done" or figurative pat on the back will be sufficient. Indeed, it's a habit well worth establishing.

47

Song (or Poetry) Recital

Generally speaking, only younger children will qualify for this activity, since inhibition or shyness seems to set in among youngsters at about the time they reach the age of ten. The point is that you should seek to enjoy your child's uninhibited nature as long as you can. And because children are learning songs, rhymes and poems as early as the age of three, they invariably delight in being furnished an opportunity to perform their talents.

The next time you are in phone contact with your child, ask whether he or she has learned any new songs, rhymes, etc., since you were last in touch. If you detect some hesitancy, perhaps because of shyness, you might be prepared with a rhyme of your own. By "going first," you can break the ice. This will often make it easier for a youngster, who might then feel sufficiently secure to give it a try.

After your child performs, be sure to respond with applause and words of praise. You might also ask your child about how the song or rhyme was learned. In other words, conduct a sort of interview. Vanity, you will find, is not limited to adults. Kids relish the attention, too.

48

Friends Saying "Hello"

If a friend(s) stops by at the time you normally have your periodic phone talk with your child, there exists the possibility of a "guest appearance."

Try to arrange the calling time on that day to coincide with when your visitor(s) will be comfortably seated in your home. Be sure to first ask whether they would enjoy saying "hello" to your child via long distance. Naturally, it is assumed that only persons with whom your child is familiar would be invited for such a purpose.

Often, your friends may have children of their own with whom your child is acquainted. This is even better yet, as kids receive a thrill from speaking with another youngster under such conditions. It's especially so if the youngsters are of similar age and sex, and if they have shared experiences together in the past. If it helps, imagine yourself as the host of a TV celebrity interview show, and put your creativity to work.

Use extension telephones and perhaps try simulating a news program. Lead off with yourself as anchorman, then a voice of a youngster comes in and says, "This is Bobby reporting from the master bedroom" or "This is Robin reporting from deep down in the basement recreation room," etc. Remember that creativity is the key to the success of such phone conversations.

49

Swapping Jokes

When two children meet for the first time, you'll find a high probability that they will take steps to become acquainted by swapping jokes. In many ways, it's comparable to adults talking about the weather. Above all, it's a good start toward forming new friendships.

Somehow, it seems, children often have a better capacity for remembering new jokes than adults. As a result, I find it helpful to jot down a few key words on a piece of scrap paper whenever I hear a worthwhile joke suitable for repeating to youngsters. The problem is, however, that I seldom hear enough such jokes over the span of a week or two to fill the demand during periodic phone calls to my son. And, sometimes I forget to jot them down.

So a librarian friend directed me to the juvenile area of the public library, where I found several monthly magazines published exclusively for children. Each magazine contained a special page where no less than a half-dozen jokes were printed. It's easy to make copies on the library copy machine.

Almost all public libraries maintain a stock of back issues of magazines, which are available on request, if they are not found directly on the shelves. With a few coins and several back issues of one or more of the kids' magazines, you should be able to supply yourself with a solid backlog of good jokes.

And don't forget to ask your child to share his or her new jokes with you.

50

Save on Phone Bills

More than a decade has passed since the court-ordered breakup of the Bell Telephone System. This government action opened new territory for competing long-distance phone services, many of which can save you money, depending on your individual needs.

Because rates and services offered change frequently, it would be impractical to attempt to pinpoint exactly which service can save you more. The best advice is to request information containing toll costs from each of the major companies and compare these with your calling needs. For example, one company might offer lower costs for calls made during weekday business hours, but their weekend rates (when you make most of your calls) might be higher than those of another company. Or one company might allow you to use their services when you travel, without extra cost, while another one doesn't.

If most of your long-distance calls to your children are placed on weekends, then it's important to shop for the best weekend rate. Also, be sure to ask whether there is a minimum use fee or a monthly service charge.

Almost all of the long-distance phone companies maintain toll-free 800 numbers which you can call to request free information. Be a careful shopper and compare, compare, compare!

51

Ham Radio

Even though you or your child don't own a ham radio outfit, most of which are rather expensive and require considerable knowledge to operate, you can nevertheless benefit.

First, locate an amateur operator in your area, either a friend or perhaps someone recommended by a friend. Explain to the ham operator that you have a son or daughter living in a distant city, and that you would like to talk with them via radio. Since there exists no restriction on third-party communications over amateur radio airwaves within the United States, the ham operator will likely seek to contact a ham living in your child's area. (Note: Many foreign countries impose restrictions on, or totally ban all third-party amateur radio traffic.)

Once radio contact has been established by the two ham operators, there are two ways to communicate with your child—either by direct contact (meaning that you are seated at the microphone at your friend's amateur radio set and your child is seated at the ham operator's set in his or her own town), or through a telephone patch setup. This is accomplished by each ham operator connecting their telephones to their equipment, after contact has been established, enabling you and your child to converse via the combined elements of phone and radio.

And, if each of you should someday manage to operate ham radio sets of your own, there would be virtually no limit to your opportunities for free long-distance talks.

52

Business Tips, Ideas, Advice

Someday, if not already, your child will reach the age when he or she decides it's time to earn money of his or her own. Though baby-sitting and newspaper routes are among the most common part-time jobs for youngsters, there exist many more. These include gardening, production and sale of handcrafted items, hauling old newspapers, vending cold lemonade, car-washing, window-cleaning, selling tree-ripened fruit, etc.

Should your son or daughter express an interest in earning money through part-time work, but lack ideas, you can be of help by offering suggestions and support. Once they get their business started, you can be available to offer advice for managing their operations, improving efficiency and then carefully investing their income.

Also, you'll discover that many youngsters nowadays are seeking introduction to the world of finance and securities at earlier ages—usually not because their parents have urged them to do so, but rather as a result of their own curiosity. It is no longer uncommon to see a youngster of 11 or 12 years of age researching and investing in the stock market.

My own personal policy has been to be available to answer questions that a child may have in such areas, to always offer encouragement, but never to coax them into ordinarily adult business ventures before they are ready to give up their bicycles and roller skates.

53

Pet Talk

If your child is like most youngsters, he or she will probably own a pet of some type. If not, it's a safe bet that your youngster would like to have a pet of his or her own.

Because pets make interesting conversation topics even among adults, this is an area you will likely wish to explore during your periodic phone talks. Within that topic, training and grooming are subjects frequently covered, and undoubtedly your child will want to share with you various experiences. You, too, will likely have some stories of your own to share with your child.

Any suggestions you can pass along to your youngster with regard to care and grooming of his or her animal will be welcome.

If you should discover a book detailing steps for the training, care and management of their special pet, it would serve as a fine gift.

And if your youngster doesn't own a pet, and expresses a desire to have one of his or her own, you should try to do what you can—within limits established by current living situations—to enable them to reach that goal.

54

Library Visits

All too often nowadays, because of TV and other electronic entertainments, children miss the opportunity to enjoy the knowledge and wonderful experiences to be discovered through the printed word. And while fewer families may even know the location of their local library, there remains nevertheless a solid core of parents who realize the importance of books in their children's lives and futures.

Most youngsters, once they have visited a public library, will eagerly look forward to the adventure of weekly visits, and will seek to take home the maximum number of books allowed. If you aren't familiar with what's available for your child at a public library, arrange to visit the one nearest you and inspect the surroundings. Look in on the children's section and observe the bulletin boards listing the numerous related activities offered. You'll find most of them are free of charge.

And though you can't accompany your child, you should encourage him or her to frequent the neighborhood library. If the custodial parent is unable to take them, attempt to arrange some alternative to enable such visits.

During your weekly phone talks, ask your youngster to tell you what he or she discovered at the library during the last visit, and inquire about what they have recently read or are reading. If you have an opportunity, try to gain access to a copy of same, and report back to your child your own impressions. Also, you might wish to recommend to your youngster any interesting books at their level that you might have recently read or learned about.

A final tip: It can't hurt to make friends with the children's librarian at your neighborhood library and check with that person periodically to inquire what's new among youngsters' reading interests.

55

Sharing Letters

As simple as the title appears, sharing with your child letters which you receive can be interesting and informative to them.

Suppose, for instance, that you receive a letter from an uncle or aunt with whom your youngster is familiar, or perhaps the parents of a child who your son or daughter knows. You will likely want to pass along to your child the highlights of the letter's content, if not read the letter aloud in its entirety. The letter will be of particular interest to your youngster if the writer is either a relative, another youngster or if the letter refers to your child.

Use your judgment in determining what portions will be of interest to your child. Occasionally, if there should be great interest expressed in one of the letters you mention, it might be a good idea to mail a copy to your child.

56

Computer Connection

As more American families add multimedia personal computers to the already widening list of electronic appliances in their homes, the greater the potential to share a part of this popular, if not necessary, technology with your child.

Personal computers serve a host of functions, as many of you reading this already know. In addition to being used for accounting, word processing, educational programs and data base operations, personal computers provide access to the Internet and the world of cyberspace. This includes e-mail, fax, electronic games and much, much more.

One of the many advantages of using electronic mail is that messages can be transmitted cheaply during all hours. And since the transmissions are generally silent, there's no chance of disturbing anyone in the receiving household. Of course, each home needs to be outfitted with a computer terminal and a modem which connects to a telephone line, enabling transmission of electronic messages.

Experts say that in the next ten years we will witness a further tremendous growth in the field of telecommunications, in which the computer will play a major role. As a result, these advances will enable parent and child to expand their relationships using communications tools which we might never have dreamed would someday exist.

57

Applause, Applause, Applause

How many people do you know for whom it seems easier to hand out hundred-dollar bills than to offer a few words of praise or congratulations?

While social trends seem to be moving toward a direction of increased communication and openness among people, there hasn't been any noticeable upswing in expression of appreciation or approval. Perhaps there's even become a noticeable lack of such applauding actions.

Because it's not usually in human nature for individuals to seek or ask for such approval, many of us become defensive or reserved in our attitudes. To help your child avoid taking such a direction, you can counteract this seeming trend by showing your generosity with words of encouragement, praise and approval at every opportunity. In short, this means providing your youngster with a verbal pat on the back, without necessary prompting, whenever you can.

You'll find it's really not difficult to find a legitimate reason to applaud some action of your son or daughter. Mostly, it will be right there in front of you, and you need only recognize it.

Quite often, youngsters only seem to hear from adults when they have something critical to say. If your approach offers a departure, it's not hard to guess whether your child will appreciate the gesture.

58

School Supplies

As an attractive briefcase can sometimes be an object of conversation between businessmen or women, so can a trendy notebook cover among the school-age set. Shiny, vinyl looseleaf notebook binders featuring color photos of a rock group, teen-age idol or a pro football team's official emblem or star player indeed make super back-to-school gifts.

Try shopping around at a drugstore, supermarket or discount store, and you'll encounter a wide assortment of such binders. Cover photo topics also depict various animals, outdoor activity scenes, movie stars and sports cars. Ask your youngster to cite a few of his or her favorites for you, and proceed from there. Remember, your child will be carrying around the new notebook binder throughout the school year and beyond. And there's a possibility it will serve as a reminder of you while you are miles away.

Other types of novelty school supply items occasionally make their debut also. If you manage to keep on top of such developments through your contacts, you can be right there to fill a need when it occurs.

59

Planting Seeds

Those little seeds which come in the brightly-colored packets can provide the start of an exciting adventure for you and your child. Easily mailed, the inexpensive supply of garden seeds come in all types and varieties. Colorful flowers, garden vegetables, fruits—all are available for planting.

Besides enjoying the experience of planting and watching the seeds grow into living plants, your son or daughter can report to you periodically on the progress of what he or she has planted. You can ask questions, provide tips and assist in solving problems of irrigation, fertilizing, control of garden pests, etc., and offer lots of encouragement. Words of praise for a job well done are always welcome.

Occasionally, your youngster might choose to send you a few sample seeds of a garden plant that he or she has successfully grown. If you plant them, you might set an example by taking color photographs of the seedlings at intervals, and continue the process until they are full-grown plants. Mail the snapshots to your child as they become available, and discuss the progress of your plants with your youngster. At a later time, your youngster might wish to send you photos of his or her plants, which, of course, should also be encouraged.

Keep your kids busy with such activities, and they will become accustomed to taking responsibility.

Children's Theater

There are few youngsters of pre-school and kindergarten age who wouldn't respond with excitement if offered an invitation to attend a live stage fairy-tale theater performance.

Cinderella, Jack and the Beanstalk, Rumpelstiltskin and *The Princess and the Pea* are among favorites often produced by children's theater groups. In most communities in the United States, there are theater groups which regularly stage such productions, mostly on weekend afternoons. Many offer season subscription tickets at discounted rates.

It is likely that for your child, who has grown up in a generation of TV and video electronics, exposure to the live stage will be a new and marvelous experience. Many youngsters who become involved in drama group activities later in high school received their introduction through attending a performance of children's theater.

Though it might take an amount of inquiring on your part, your child will undoubtedly appreciate it if you can arrange for him or her to attend children's theater. If they like what they see, you might later talk about the possibility of arranging for a season's subscription.

Working out the logistics of attending these stage performances may also require some organizing (such as whether your former spouse, or an adult relative or friend will accompany your child), but you'll know it was worth your effort when you receive the feedback.

61

A Child's Own Room

When coming for a visit with you, having his or her own bedroom will help make your child feel further secure.

This doesn't entail simply ushering your youngster to a guest bedroom and saying, "Here's your room." It means, instead, that you outfit and decorate a room—meanwhile seeking your child's input and suggestions—the same as you would if your child were living with you year-round.

It's important for your children to know that they have a place in your home, and that it's there waiting for them whenever they come.

During a phone conversation, you might sometimes say that a certain item, etc. arrived for them, and that you will put it in *their room*, even if they might not be coming back to your home for several months.

Of course, it's not always possible for every parent to provide a private bedroom for every child. Such might be the ideal, but there exist numerous creative ways to establish the same or a similar feeling without the ability to offer an individual room.

Once again, imagination becomes an important ingredient in such circumstances. Use it.

62

Greetings From Us All

Why is it that so often we only see the names of children who are part of two-parent households appearing on holiday greeting cards? Single parents can and should include the names of their children, whether or not the youngsters are living in their home.

Too often, a non-custodial mother or father feels embarrassed and is hesitant to include his or her children on such greeting cards, seeing themselves perhaps as something less than those friends and acquaintances of theirs who remain married.

A father I know, who spends summers with his son and daughter, annually chooses a "family" photograph taken during a scenic outing that year for his Christmas photo-greeting. He, his son and his daughter are always in the picture, together as a family. The greeting card is produced for him by a photo chain store which offers a wide selection of such greetings.

There are many such stores in most locations throughout the United States. You need only furnish the photo. The store will take care of the rest, including the lettering for the greeting card, envelopes, etc.

63

Apricots, Pears, Plums

Almost anywhere you live, there will be a season during which a locally grown fruit or vegetable is harvested. Many of these farm or orchard products are also simultaneously canned, dried, preserved or made into jellies.

Your youngster will delight if you remember him or her when these seasons come along by sending a small package of whatever specialty crop is grown and packaged in your area. Typical examples are dried apricots in California, tart cherry jam in Wisconsin, canned kumquats in Florida, maple syrup in Vermont, and many more.

If you are relatively new in your area, learn what is grown there and what is available for shipping during various seasons. Then try them out on your youngster and find out which ones he or she enjoys most.

It's a safe bet that you will soon find a return customer for one or more of these annual delights.

64

Conference Calls

Mostly common to the business executive, the conference phone call is something that you might wish to use on special occasions. While such long-distance calls are expensive, there may be certain events when the expense is worthwhile.

Such an instance might be when your child is celebrating a birthday or has reached some important milestone, perhaps religious, academic, or athletic. It may also be that relatives on your side of the family, living in other cities, want to join with you in wishing your youngster well.

Another situation could involve the arrival of a good friend or relative from a foreign country. Such a person might find himself or herself in the United States for only a brief stay, and is unable to visit either you or your child due to business schedules. Suppose that you live in Los Angeles, your child resides in Chicago and the relative is staying for only two days in New York before returning home. A conference call might be the solution.

There exist numerous other opportunities for reaping the benefits of a conference call, and, of course, these depend on individual needs. It should be cautioned that you check in advance with your long-distance telephone company to determine the rates before setting up such a call.

65

Matching Your Sports Forecasts

Will the Yankees beat the Dodgers? Which team will win the Super Bowl? Who will be top finisher in the U.S. Open?

As your child finds himself or herself becoming interested in sports events, you will soon find yourself being challenged to pick a team against a favorite team of your youngster's choosing.

Once it begins, the friendly rivalry is likely to continue the year around, what with major-league baseball, basketball, football and golf events regularly telecast over network and cable TV. Necessarily, this will also bring up an issue for parental discretion—that of whether it is appropriate to allow a child to bet, even though it might be only a dime or a quarter, and the bet is strictly between parent and child. This will be a matter for individual decision, and it's possible that a creative parent, who doesn't approve of wagering, might dream up a substitute method that allows the challenge and competition to exist without the wager.

While my son and I would often bet a quarter on a nationally televised game, we would also delight in holding a "draft" when it came to the major televised golf events of the year. We would flip a coin to decide who chose first. Then, alternately, each would select six leading golfers. Whichever of the dozen golfers finished closest to the top of the tournament would be declared the winner between us. If one of the golfers we chose didn't play in the tournament or failed to make the cut, it was ruled a misfortune, but there were no further alternate choices permitted.

The betting was never allowed to get out of hand. Mostly, the debts were kept recorded on a slip of paper, and by year's end there was seldom more than a few cents difference to be settled.

66

Critic's Award

When your child reaches the age of interest in coloring books and crayons, you can expect a new dimension to be added to your relationship. You may term it "art appreciation."

And when you next send your son or daughter a coloring book, be sure it's the kind that has pages which are easily removable. Also, send your former spouse a supply of stamped, self-addressed envelopes, explaining your wish that the pictures be mailed to you. Ask your youngster to send you his or her completed colorings, using the envelopes provided. Obviously, children under the age of 5 or 6 years will require assistance from an adult in mailing.

After you have received the initial mailing, mention in your next phone call that you received it and that you enjoyed looking at each picture. Take the time to appreciate each of the colorings, and perhaps make a few notes as to your reactions. Tell your child how much you enjoyed seeing his or her coloring work, detailing what you liked about each picture. Let your child know that you took the time to look at them, and encourage your youngster to send you more.

Be generous with your praise. There's no need to be false or artificial—there are plenty of good things you can discern in your children's colored pictures. Let them know. And let's keep those pages coming!

67

Special Order Photos

If your son or daughter follows a favorite sports team or musical group or dance company, etc., you can be a winner.

All you need do is write the team or group's office and ask from where or whom you can order individual photos or postcard-style photos of its members. Often, a commercial photographer or firm holds an exclusive franchise for such photos and will send you a price list upon request. In other instances, the team or group's office handles such requests directly.

My son was a fan of the Oakland A's, and I wrote the team's office requesting such information. I was referred to a commercial photographer, who produced color postcards of most of the team's members. The cards were reasonably priced and I ordered a complete set, spacing them apart by mailing them to my son at the rate of about one a month. As new players were added to the team, the photographer made new postcards for each one, meanwhile informing his customers of same.

The field is not limited to sports, however. Add to the list ballet company members, national parks, horses, dogs, birds, other entertainment stars and so forth.

Discover your child's interest and apply your imagination. You will find there exists no limitation to what you can accomplish.

68

Itinerary Briefing

During summer vacations, or at other times, you will likely have an opportunity to travel with your child. You can make such trips more interesting by furnishing your youngster with an itinerary several weeks in advance of your departure. And if your child has already reached the fifth or sixth grade in school, it will offer a challenge if you ask him or her to prepare a brief, thumbnail description of the places you intend to visit.

When my son and I traveled via train from Oakland, California, to Chicago on the San Francisco Zephyr, a two-day trip, I requested from Amtrak a brochure containing information about the train's route and the cities along the way as well as locations of natural interest and historical sites. I also obtained from the American Automobile Association a large map of the United States. Between the map, brochure and a timetable—all of which I mailed to my son—he was able to inform himself on what he might expect to encounter. By the time we finally got under way, he knew almost as well as the train's crew what stops lay along the route and what time we were scheduled to arrive at each. Knowing these facts served to heighten his level of anticipation and enjoyment. Naturally, we were also well equipped with games to pass the time between stops.

As a child moves into the upper grades in school, such trips can also prove worthwhile as class projects. Of course, your child must ask the teacher for approval. The project could include a hand-drawn map, timetable and a well-researched description of the points along the route.

69

Golf and Tennis Tips

Before you know it, your son or daughter will reach the age where he or she becomes interested in tennis or golf among other sports.

Sharing your knowledge or background in these sports can prove valuable for your youngster's development while installing yet another common bond in your relationship. In addition to drawing on your own experiences, you'll find numerous opportunities to clip suggestions and strategy tips from newspapers and magazines. Send these in the mail to your child, and later ask for feedback.

Also, you might occasionally discover a paperback book authored by an outstanding golfer or tennis player on improving one's game. Your youngster would welcome such a gift.

Meanwhile, make certain that the exchange doesn't get too far out of balance. Keep in mind that your child should also furnish you with an account of his or her own experiences.

Remember, it's give-and-take that makes for a good relationship.

70

Studying for Exams

When a child receives a final semester grade with which he or she isn't satisfied, it is often a reflection of the student's performance on the final examination or on a key mid-term test.

If you ask your youngster to detail how he or she prepared for the exam, you will likely hear a description of something less than an organized approach.

Emphasize to your child that he or she is no less intelligent or capable than any other youngster in the class and that like other youngsters, your child can also receive a good or excellent grade. To do so, however, your child must understand that a major part of the final grade is tied to the exam(s), and that *how* to prepare for those exams is the secret to success.

To begin, your child must take notes during the course, read the assigned material and underline those items to which the teacher applies emphasis. Often, a teacher will review for an exam or will indicate what material the exam will cover. Once this is known, your child should take the material home, review what is to be covered—by skimming, not attempting to reread each word—and in doing so use paper clips to accent the items likely to be included in the exam.

Next, your child should locate a classmate who is willing to spend not less than two hours "drilling" for the exam. This should be done in the afternoon or evening (*not* late at night) prior to the day the exam is to be given. Each child should take turns quizzing the other, covering all of the material and repeating later those questions which were not promptly or confidently answered during the first round.

When the material appears to have been mastered by both students, the study session is completed. Generally, a treat, such as a soda or a snack, is appropriate, which also affords time for the classmates to further discuss the exam, though in a more relaxed atmosphere.

Upon awakening the next morning, your youngster should once again browse over the material covered the night before, especially focusing on those items that are not yet within complete recall grasp. At this point, it's effective to use whatever aid technique helps to get the material established in one's mind. If, for example, it is necessary to remember for a local history exam that the early founders of a community were Frank Jones, Hiram Stewart and Martha Bradbourne, it can help to remember three persons with whom the exam taker is familiar, such as a Frank, a Martha and a person named Stewart or Stuart (since it is unlikely that anyone will be personally acquainted with a Hiram). Such associations often help someone to remember names over a short term. This technique is commonly known as a mnemonic device.

Finally, immediately prior to taking the exam, your child should quickly run over the material in the same manner as reviewed during the early morning.

Bet you there will be improvement, if your child follows the steps.

71

Little League Scoreboard

When your youngster, whether a boy or a girl, is part of a Little League baseball team, on-field performance becomes a matter of great importance. The number of hits, fielding plays and strikeouts (if your child is a pitcher) will immediately become the subject of any conversation, if you chance to ask—and even if you don't.

You will find what will please your Little Leaguer to no end is your taking the time to ask for a copy of his or her season's schedule sometime prior to the official start. Then, during each weekend's phone conversation, ask for a recap of the week's Little League activities, simultaneously noting the scores and the personal highlights of your child's games. This will provide you with a ready reference and also be available, should your youngster want you to help calculate his or her batting average. It's also important to keep informed of the team's standing in the league and also the status of the team in season-end playoffs.

Being a well-informed Little League parent tells your child that you care. Remember, it's those little things that count most.

72

Scouting Builds

The Boy Scouts and Girl Scouts have helped to develop young men and women for almost a century. It will be to your child's advantage if he or she is a part of the movement. You can help by encouraging your youngster to take part in scouting activities and to earn proficiency in various hobbies and special interests.

Those most active often receive badges upon completion of a special project or mini-course of study. Ask your child during your conversations which particular badge he or she is attempting to earn. Ask what is being done to reach the goal, what supplies are needed, difficulties encountered, etc. You can often help, without being there, if only to offer approval and encouraging words. Occasionally, your youngster might need a particular item for scouting, which you can usually find available in your own town at a store which carries either scouting equipment or outdoor supplies. Such makes a fine gift and is certain to be appreciated.

Get involved with your youngster's scouting activities. You'll be glad you did.

73

Mediating Disputes

There will come times when your child or children find themselves faced with conflicts which they can't handle alone. And though attempting to resolve such conflicts or disputes—by telephone—isn't the easiest task, your assistance can often prove quite valuable.

Typical examples are cases where one youngster won't allow the other to use his or her this or that. In such instances, you might want to mediate the dispute by discussing the matter with the children, one at a time. If the conflict is between the youngster and the custodial parent, then again, a separate discussion with each of the parties is advised. Often, such discussions might require switching back and forth several times between the parties—"shuttle diplomacy," it's often been termed—until a resolution can be reached.

Initially bringing all the parties together at one time through the use of extension telephones serves no purpose as a means of achieving resolution. It is sometimes a valuable tool to use *after* agreement has been reached. At such time, getting everyone together on the phone and explaining the terms of the agreement can be quite useful. It enables you to ask each party to the agreement whether they understand the terms and agree to abide by them. Also, ask each party to cite the terms back to you so that there can be no misunderstanding.

74

For the Science-Minded

This won't fit every youngster, but if your child is interested in science, it might indeed prove a bonanza.

The Smithsonian Institution offers a variety of science kits for youngsters according to age groups. For example, there's an Art and Science of Creativity kit for children beginning at age five. Also Scientific Explorer kits, such as the Science of Taste and the Science of Sound for ages eight and older. Or a Crystal Growing kit for children ages ten and older.

The kits can be ordered shipped directly to your child. To receive a catalog and ordering information, write:

> Smithsonian Catalog
> Department 0006
> Washington, D.C. 20073

In requesting the catalog, please add that you would like to receive future mailings about available new science kits and other similar offerings.

Meanwhile, contact with any science teacher (it needn't be your child's teacher) can help you find other useful hints and ideas.

75

Private Lessons

Though mention of this subject immediately brings to mind the grimacing youngster who is required to take piano lessons, there's also a different side to the picture. It's the child who has an unquenchable desire to learn drawing, painting, ballet, drama, golf, horseback riding, tennis, singing or to play a musical instrument. The youngster's ambitions are many, while, unfortunately, too often the opportunities to realize them are few.

Every parent will have his or her own approach to this situation, as I have mine: If a youngster expresses an interest in taking any kind of lessons, my reply is that I will be pleased to help. Note that the word is *help*—not completely bankroll. I would say to a child, "If you want clarinet lessons (or baton training or riding lessons), you must demonstrate a willingness to make an investment of your own." I suggest further that the interested youngster either earn some money by baby-sitting, performing chores, cutting lawns, etc. The amount or percentage the youngster contributes toward his or her lessons is not important. Rather, it's the fact that he or she makes any contribution at all—and from earned money. And, if the youngster shows a

willingness to work, I would have no reluctance to go as far as the federal government sometimes does and provide 90 percent of the funds needed while the recipient of the lessons pays the remaining 10 percent.

If you haven't considered this approach before, give it a try.

76

Grade Reports

When it's time for the school to send home your child's report card, you will want to discuss it with your youngster.

Simply ask your son or daughter to make a photocopy of the grade report and mail it to you. This can be facilitated by sending in advance a stamped, self-addressed envelope and a few coins for the copy machine. Ordinarily coin-operated copy machines can be found in supermarkets, post offices, discount stores and other public places. Also, advise your child that there is always a coin-fed copy machine in the nearest public library.

When you have your youngster's report in hand, discuss it with him or her, but never allow yourself to appear angry or upset. If your child's grades have slipped, ask what might be the cause. Be understanding and try to help. You need not be satisfied with lowered grades, but at the same time, getting on your child's case won't help, either. Take a constructive approach and deal with the issue as you would any other problem. You might offer workable suggestions and incentives. And don't wait until the next grade report is issued. Instead, try to monitor your child's progress week by week. This way, you can determine whether your youngster is following through with his or her declared plan for improvement.

And when the grades denote superior work or reflect improvement, it's time for reinforcement. First, give your child that verbal "well done" via phone, and then follow with a gift, making explicitly known its purpose—a reward for outstanding effort.

77

Home Recipes

Yet another way to share experiences via long distance is through the exchange of recipes.

Have you been invited to a friend's home and discovered an entree that you've never tasted before? Or a simply super dessert? Ask your host or hostess to allow you to jot down the recipe, and then send a copy of it off to your daughter—or perhaps, your son.

Also, encourage your child to send you his or her favorite recipe. It's great fun to report back a few weeks later, telling how you tried a certain dish and detailing your experiences. At the same time, you can enjoy hearing from your youngster about the recipe you sent and whether it was as delicious as you yourself found it.

Exchanging recipes is easy to accomplish, and it's always good food for discussion.

78

Telegram!

A wire or mailgram is a means of communication that should be reserved for special occasions. Though you won't use it often, there are those events for which you'll be glad you did.

Examples are messages wishing good luck when your son or daughter is entered in a sports competition or perhaps the opening-night performance of a theater production in which he or she is involved. And, of course, congratulatory messages, too. These are most appreciated in instances where a youngster has been chosen to receive an award or honor.

Though it costs more than a long-distance call, a telegram is something that can be kept and looked at again and again over the years.

Imagination and discretion will tell you when it's appropriate to employ this powerful medium. Use it sparingly, but when you go for it, make it count!

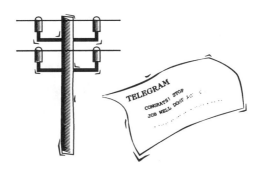

79

What's Today's Date?

Almost every youngster's room has a calendar mounted on the wall or closet door. There are those adorned with Walt Disney animal characters, National Football League stars, horses, nature scenes, photos of foreign lands, rock groups, movieland characters, etc.

Whichever your child's interest, there exists an appropriate calendar. And since they are likely to glance at it every day, they will be reminded of your presence.

Over the years, I sent my son numerous types of calendars. The one he liked best for the most years was one that featured color photos of key buildings and monuments in the nation's capital. Printed each year by the U.S. Capitol Historical Society, the calendar is often found in government offices, classrooms and other locations where it receives prominent display.

However, chances are that your child's interest will run to other areas, including sports, music, animals, etc. Best bet is to determine your youngster's favorite area of interest and then set about investigating the various possibilities for obtaining and mailing an appropriate calendar. If you have difficulty and can't find a direct source, try visiting a stationery or greeting card store or gift shop. They often feature a sizable line of assorted novelty or theme calendars.

Most are in stock mid to late October.

Say It With Flowers

If you have a daughter, there will be those special occasions when sending flowers is just the right thing.

Beginning with graduation from kindergarten or a first recital in a ballet class, there are events that afford you an opportunity to express to your child that you care. Sometimes, the occasion might be only that your daughter is being taken by family members or friends to a restaurant, the theater or an opera. In such instance, a small corsage would be most appreciated. Later on, there will be school dances, receiving honors or possibly a hospitalization for removal of tonsils or appendix, during which delivery of flowers brings with it your message.

Flowers can be ordered through your neighborhood florist. And if you don't have the name of a reliable florist in your daughter's town, then often sending flowers by wire is the best way. However, if you can locate a florist within proximity of your daughter's home, you will frequently do best to patronize such a florist directly.

Once you have established contact with the florist in your daughter's town, you need not regularly telephone, but instead mail your request—well in advance—and enclose a check for the amount you wish to spend. In doing so, you eliminate the need for long-distance tolls, commissions paid to the referring florist in your town and the credit-card charge paid by the florist. As a result, I've found your recipient often receives a higher quality selection because the florist isn't required to split with anyone the amount you are paying.

And, of course, virtually all florists will deliver your order.

81

Easter Bunny

Special cards for Easter, mailed ahead a week or more, are quite important to remind your child that you are thinking of him or her on the holiday. However, finding a suitable approach to observe Easter with your youngster poses a challenge.

Sure, you simply send an Easter basket, you say? Have you recently tried sending dyed, hard-boiled eggs through the mail?

But there is yet a way. If you have friends or acquaintances in your child's town, they can help. Meanwhile, you write the card to go with the basket, discuss with your friends what you might place in the basket and hope it all works out. And whatever you do, be sure to send your friends a note of thanks. There is no substitute for expressed appreciation. Also, there's next year to think about, too.

If you don't know anyone in the area who can arrange the basket and its delivery, there's another possibility. Telephone the chamber of commerce in that area and attempt to make contact with someone in the office who you sense cares. Be persistent, though polite. Ask if there are any gift stores or package-wrapping services in the town that might undertake such a request. Or, as a last chance, perhaps a florist.

Then call to find the shop that will do it for you. If you keep trying, you'll find someone.

82

Trick or Treat

What shall I be on Halloween? A ghost? A witch? A pirate? Such questions are on the minds of youngsters during the weeks in early fall, when the days grow shorter.

Discussing the various costume possibilities with your child can be both helpful and fun. Seek to encourage creativity and resourcefulness rather than the purchase of a ready-made costume, especially if your youngster is old enough to put together his or her own.

A couple of weeks before Halloween, visit a specialty card shop and select a suitable Halloween card for your child. Before mailing, you might attempt to find available gift-certificate coupons sold by either nationwide hamburger or ice-cream chains in your area. Such coupons are often available in smaller denominations and are accepted throughout the country. (Once, I was fortunate enough to find some that had been printed by a hamburger chain especially as a Halloween trick-or-treat gift.) Then enclose either the coupons or, if unavailable, a few dollars as your gift to your child.

Try to phone your youngster the day or evening before Halloween. Inquire whether the card and gift arrived, and ask your child to describe his or her costume. It's usually best not to phone on Halloween night, as your child will be quite excited and things will be busy.

When you talk with your child again on the following weekend, be sure to ask him or her to tell you of their Halloween experiences, what types of trick-or-treat goodies he or she received, etc., and to send you an in-costume photo, if available.

Halloween can be a fun time for both you and your little goblin, even when you can't be together.

83

April Fool!

You have a full 365 days between jokes or pranks to dream up a new one for this once-a-year event. There's a full assortment of April Fool's humor, and your own collection from past years will likely serve best.

You might consider something like this: When you talk with your child on the weekend before April Fool's Day—assuming April 1 doesn't fall on a weekend—you mention that a friend of yours, named Mr. Wolf or Mr. Fox, will be visiting in your youngster's town on, let's say Thursday (if that's April Fool's Day), and that this person will have a message to deliver to your child. Then, furnish your youngster with the phone number of the local area zoo, explaining that Mr. Fox or Mr. Wolf can be reached at that phone number. Suggest that your youngster phone Mr. Fox or Mr. Wolf to arrange for delivery of the special message.

When your youngster phones the number and discovers it's that of the zoo, he or she will catch on quickly. Of course, the next time you speak with your child thereafter, you'll have to explain that it was all an April Fool's joke.

But, be careful! Your child might soon learn to turn the tables around, and then the joke will be on you.

84

Tongue Twisters

Betcha can't say. "Rubber buggy bumpers," three times, real fast!

Kids love tongue twisters, and whenever you phone your youngster, he or she will be delighted to give it a try, if you offer the challenge.

The best place to build a resource is the children's area of your public library. If you can't locate a book or monthly magazine with tongue twisters, just ask the librarian for help. And remember, the copy machine in the library can be your convenient friend.

Here's a stumper you can save for that day when your child begins to believe that he or she is the best tongue twister sayer in the land: "The sun shines on Shoshanah's sewing shop signs."

85

A Place for Those Placemats

Next time you eat in a restaurant, you might glance at the placemat in front of you.

If it's paper, there will often be a message or promotion of some kind printed on its face. Sometimes it's a map, or perhaps a sports quiz or nostalgia questions, etc. Large fast-food chains are particularly well-known for the unique types of placemats used, and change them frequently, whenever offering a new promotion.

My son is a sports fan, so I was always sure to pick up any placemat (only paper ones, of course) that were connected with sports or sports knowledge.

Naturally, the placemat went into the weekly mailing to my youngster.

86

Make Mine Music

Did you ever buy a CD or cassette you wanted to share with your child? Or perhaps you recently heard some music on radio or TV you felt was something special?

Why not share with your child via long-distance? You assume the role of the disc jockey, and at a later time, perhaps your youngster will be the DJ, and you the listener.

Next time you wish to share music, prepare by hooking up your CD or cassette player near the phone, or vice versa. Unless you're an electronics whiz and can arrange for a direct feed into the equipment, place the phone receiver on a pillow where the sound from the speaker can be easily picked up. If the music was heard on radio or TV, you will have already recorded it on your cassette, and it's ready for playing.

Since the time length of such music is often more than a few minutes' duration, you might wish to transmit only the highlight portions to your child. Explain that the entire CD or cassette can be played (or repeated) when your child comes to visit you. And, if the selected music proves to be a real winner with your youngster, you might consider mailing him or her the CD or cassette as a gift.

87

Bedtime Stories

For youngsters between the ages of approximately three and nine years (obviously, there are no set limits—it depends on each individual youngster), bedtime stories often highlight an important part of their day.

A child who is told or read bedtime stories experiences an inner sense of security, a feeling that he or she is loved and cared about.

Though you can't do it every evening, it might be possible to work out an arrangement where you phone once a week, in addition to your regular weekend "visit," so that you may share a bedtime story with your child. If there is a phone in the child's room, that's an added convenience. If not, perhaps one can be moved there for a few minutes, either a portable phone or by using a long extension cord. Under all circumstances, you should have an agreement with your youngster that when the story is over, he or she will immediately go to bed (much the way it would be if you were at home with your child).

Depending on your youngster's age and interests, you might either read aloud from a book of fairy tales, adventure short stories, sports milestones of the past or you may wish to tell stories from your own repertoire—perhaps tales you heard told by your parents or grandparents. And when it's time to go to sleep, you can tell your child good night, just as if you were there. It's being close, despite all the miles separating.

88

Travel Preview

The pleasure of an upcoming trip or excursion can be heightened for both you and your child through a few easy steps.

Suppose that during next summer's vacation, you and your youngster plan to visit certain parks or campgrounds in your state or neighboring states. Make a list of the places you intend to visit and promptly send off some postcards to the facilities as well as to chambers of commerce in those and surrounding areas requesting available brochures and information about attractions and places of interest. Once you have received these, parcel them out a few at a time by enclosing them in letters you send your child. Also, later, you can discuss the brochures when you talk with your child.

In past years, I have sent my son major league baseball schedules, color brochures and photocopied pages from various reference books or encyclopedia as part of setting the stage for our summer activities. As a result, when the time arrives, your child will not only

have built to a peak his or her enthusiasm, but will be informed as well—or likely, better-than any tourist or visitor whom you might encounter.

And, remember, it's not necessary that there be any major travel. If your child is coming to visit you in your home city or town, there usually exist within reasonable driving distance numerous activities for youngsters. For many of these, brochures or folders are available, and they are generally free for the asking. If some offer no brochures, keep a watch out for a newspaper article or a listing appearing in the weekend activities section of your local paper.

89

In Case of Illness

There will be those times when your youngster takes ill and you want to do something, but feel unable to do so. But you *can* do several things, and the distance won't matter.

On first report of illness or accident, send a get-well card. Don't delay. Get the card into the mailbox the same day because of the several days required for delivery. Also, follow up the next day with a phone call—it needn't be long, and often it shouldn't be—to check and see how your child is feeling.

It's a good policy to ask your former spouse how your child is progressing and whether he or she is too ill to receive a phone call. If it's not best to do so at the moment, request that your child be informed that you called to inquire about his or her condition.

Often, in the case of a not-too-serious illness, your child will answer the phone himself or herself, and you can ask your question directly. A few words of encouragement are always appreciated, as well as a reminder from you that the disorder won't be forever, etc.

In instances of a prolonged illness or an accident that results in a lengthy convalescence, such as a broken leg, you might consider mailing a get-well gift. And in those cases where a child requires hospitalization, an appropriate gift or remembrance is also advised.

96

Knowing That You Care

One of the ways in which kids are different from adults is by their plain honesty. As a consequence, subtleties often can get past youngsters, though an adult would pick up on the same immediately.

So, while you might not find it necessary to tell an adult that you care—the very fact that you telephone them via long distance implies that—kids need to be (and *want* to be) told.

When you are preparing to wind up an enjoyable conversation with your youngster, be sure to let the child know that you miss him or her, and that you care very much. It's often best not to wait for a response, as it is sometimes awkward for a child to express himself or herself in such instances. Instead, proceed with whatever you were intending to say. You'll know that your child was reassured by your words even though there might have been no direct response. Kids do need to know that their parents, though separated by distance or divorce, still love them.

However, you needn't invoke those words each and every time or, like anything else, they may lose their meaning.

91

Crossword Puzzles

Working easy crossword puzzles together doesn't take long and can be enjoyable.

The best choice for such puzzles are in publications that are sold nationally and available on most newsstands. This assures that your child and you will have access to the same puzzles.

Perhaps, the favorite crossword puzzle of many youngsters is one appearing in the weekly *TV Guide*, sold at newsstands and supermarket checkout counters everywhere. This would be a great one on which to get started with your child. Others can be found in certain sports magazines. And they are also featured in almost every children's magazine, which means that you would either have to arrange for your own copy or visit your neighborhood library and make a copy of the puzzle on a copy machine.

If your youngster knows that you plan to work the puzzle together, he or she will wait for the phone call before starting.

Give the idea a try.

92

Duplicate Game Sets

Playing table games with your child this way can be rather expensive—because of the long-distance phone bill—so the choice of whether to try it depends on your budget.

Anyway, here's how it works: determine which are among your child's favorite games. There appears to be a continuous stream of new games being introduced on the market, many of which are takeoffs on popular TV game shows. If your child already has a set, you'll need only buy one for yourself.

Next time you talk with your youngster, let him or her know that you now also have the same game as they have. Offer to play them a round, perhaps when you are scheduled to phone next. This way, they will have their game set up and ready, near the phone, when you call.

All that's required now is to start the game and proceed in a manner that can best be described as one similar to playing chess via mail. In other words, if the blue piece moves two jumps on your child's board, then you move the same piece on your board the same number of moves.

Completing a single round of a particular game might require anywhere from 20 to 45 minutes, and sometimes longer. As mentioned, it can prove quite an expensive way to enjoy playing games with your child. You will have to be the judge as to whether it's worth it.

93

Calling the Plays

If your youngster enjoys football, it can very likely become an all-or-nothing interest. Among adults, such is called an obsession. But, in youth, it's quite normal.

The men who "talk football" at your office usually cover only the weekend's National Football League activity, discuss some of the sensational action around the league and drop a lot of names.

But the youngster who is immersed in the game often wants to go beyond such preliminaries. He (or sometimes she) wants to talk complete plays, and in detail.

You can find these play diagrams in some football magazines, although seldom will they appear in a general sports publication. Your public library is also a good bet to locate them.

Make sure you both have paper and pencil in hand when you begin talking plays.

Since your child will likely seek to try out some of these plays in touch football games involving his or her neighborhood pals, you'll want to follow up in future phone conversations to determine how they worked out.

This football play stuff is something you wouldn't want to push onto your youngster, as some kids are not committed to the sport that intensely. But if your son or daughter has the football fever, then detailing plays is just what the doctor prescribed.

94

Play Tic-Tac-Toe

You can play tic-tac-toe via phone almost as easily as you could if both of you were in your living room.

Simply ask your child if he or she would like to play a few rounds, allow time for them to get a sheet of paper and a pencil and begin the game.

There's not much more to suggest, except don't make it too hard on your child if he or she is just beginning. As you know, an intelligent adult can play the game so that an opponent can never win a round, only gain a tie (or cat's game, as it's often called) sometimes.

95

Counseling Problems

Much like adults, children have their problems, too. And it's when they need help that Mom or Dad, whether at home or distant, can come to the rescue.

You'll find that being a long-distance parent makes it a little more difficult for your youngster to immediately confide to you his or her problems. But, it's not impossible, and you can prove a tower of wisdom and strength if you take patience.

It's often the case that you will have to begin by asking each time during your regular phone conversations whether everything is going all right, or how your child is getting along in school or at home. It might be necessary to remind your child, "It's okay; you can tell Dad (or Mom)..."

Certainly, good counseling techniques cannot be detailed in a short space, but then common sense—an essential ingredient—cannot be taught in a counseling manual, either. So if you allow common sense the upper hand, and meanwhile encourage your child to independently examine the different alternatives available toward solving the problem, you will have taken a major step. And be sure to offer lots of support and understanding. Let your child know that you care. This is so important that it cannot be overemphasized.

Everyone has their own style and approach to solving problems, and no matter what yours is, if it works, it's okay.

96

Improving Class Reports

Creative imagination can pay off handsomely for your child in his or her class reports if you furnish the required spark.

This holds true particularly in connection with orally delivered reports, which youngsters, beginning in the third or fourth grade, are often assigned to prepare. As you can well appreciate, many teachers—as well as students—often find themselves bored to tears after being required to hear a dozen or more such reports in the same day. So, then, why not jazz up those reports with only a little extra effort?

That's where the imagination—yours and your child's—comes into play. Suppose that your child has been assigned to prepare an oral report to the class on a foreign country or a U.S. state. Beyond research in the encyclopedia and other references, and later presenting a routine report of the facts, there is yet more that can be done.

Visual aids can be obtained, such as maps, travel posters, slides, handcrafts and agricultural products (often found in the produce section of a supermarket). Add to that currency, coins, stamps and souvenirs. Also, cultural music of a nation or region can be taped onto

a cassette recorder from CDs at a library and played during the presentation as background sound. To make the presentation even more effective, your child can pass around for individual inspection by the class some of the non-breakable items used for display purposes.

Once kids understand that such assignments need not be dull—either for themselves or for the class—a motivation for both showmanship and pride of work develops.

97

Giveaway Contests

Every time you turn around, it seems, some company or chain is offering a free prize game. The bonanzas often range from a few dollars cash prize to an all-expense paid trip for two to the Super Bowl.

Supermarket chains, airlines, newspapers, magazines and fast-food restaurants are among a few of the many businesses that seasonally embark upon such promotional gimmicks. And since kids like to collect those little cards where you scratch off the hidden numbers or symbols (using the edge of a coin, usually), it's a natural for you to team up with your child in an attempt to win a prize.

Besides the scratch-off cards, sometimes coupons will be enclosed in retail packages. Or sometimes it's necessary to register or enroll in order to be eligible. Whichever it is, you'll usually find that your son or daughter will be enthusiastic about entering contests, games or drawings in which there exists the possibility of winning a super-grand prize. However, for you and your youngster both to participate, the giveaway must be offered by either a nationwide chain or a regional one within whose boundaries you and your child live.

During all the years my son and I entered contests, the only prize that we won was a free milk shake and French fries in a contest sponsored by a hamburger chain during the Olympic Games.

However, it was fun, and that's the most important thing.

98

Keep 'Em Supplied

If you think it's a real chore for you as an adult to sit down and write a letter, you can multiply by ten to arrive at how difficult it is for your child.

A step toward making it easier for your youngster to take pen in hand is providing him or her with an adequate supply of stationery, stamps and labels. If you shop where there's a large selection, you will discover varieties and styles of stationery that you didn't dream existed. Some stationery sets carry the theme of professional football, cartoon characters, recording stars, flowers, birds, cats, dogs, horses, etc. Choose the style you feel suits your child's interest and mail it to him or her together with sufficient postage for a dozen or so mailings. For a small amount extra, you can order a supply of personalized return mailing labels printed with your child's name and address.

Once your youngster has received the supplies, make these a topic of discussion and explain that although you both visit together frequently on the phone, correspondence is a medium all its own, which needs to be learned and used.

You might remind your child that he or she is fortunate in having an opportunity to correspond, since many youngsters don't. Surveys show that large percentages of college students are unable to write a letter. Your child won't be among those, if you offer encouragement at an early age.

99

When You Were a Kid

A long-distance mother, living in Hawaii, sent us this delightful suggestion for sharing with her daughter what her own life was like when she was a youngster.

Using plain paper and a photocopy machine, she assembled a collection of photos, hand-drawn sketches, memorabilia and other childhood reminiscences, compiling them into an attractive 24-page booklet.

The booklet included photos of the mother cuddling a puppy, riding a pony and wearing a Halloween costume—all when she was a girl. The captions beneath each photo or sketch recalled favorite childhood memories. These included some of the imaginative games she played as a youngster.

You can do this yourself by putting together a list over a period of time. The list might include the places you lived as a child, names of your relatives, close friends and things you enjoyed. Then, try to gather snapshots taken during your childhood, perhaps an old scrapbook or other keepsakes. Use your creativity. You will find that you can inexpensively assemble such a booklet.

When you mail it to your youngster, just wait to hear the reaction: "You mean you did these things when you were a kid?" might be your child's first question.

100

Equal Treatment

No different than if you had them at home, fathers and mothers with two or more youngsters must take care to evenly distribute the time and energy spent with their kids.

This doesn't mean that each and every conversation, gift or effort expended in their behalf is to be measured tit-for-tat. Instead, take the time to explain to your children that there will be occasions when one might seem to be receiving more attention than the other(s), but that over the long run, it will all even out.

Meanwhile, try to keep in the back of your head a sort of loosely kept file that will let you know when you need to compensate to the child or children who seemed to have been on the short receiving end lately. And, despite your best effort, you'll find that occasionally one of your kids will pop out some remark about favoritism, such as, "Johnny (or Susie) got this or that, and I didn't."

At such times, you can remind the protesting youngster that two weeks ago he or she received this or that, and Johnny (or Susie) didn't. Or that he or she spent 20 minutes talking about a TV program, using a major portion of the long-distance phone time, while the other brother (or sister) didn't.

101

As Near as the Phone

Much as it's painful, your child will sometimes feel it necessary to tell you that he or she wishes that the two of you could be together. Or perhaps that you and Mom (or Dad) could be together again.

These are indeed difficult expressions to cope with, much less attempt to address. But kids do need answers, and preferably ones that are both informative and meaningful to them. Some divorced parents handle this by explaining that it isn't possible right now to be together, but that this coming summer (or Christmas or Easter vacation or birthday) you *will* be getting together, at the same time emphasizing that such a time is only so many weeks or months away. And that in terms of a year, that's only a short time. Why, you can almost count the days!

Partings after a visit are also difficult, and often evoke similar questions. In such instances, a positive approach centers on using those last few minutes to discuss what you both plan to do during the next visit and how that time is just around the corner.

Meanwhile, be sure to remind your child that you would like to be with him or her all the time, but since that's not possible right now, you are always as near as the phone or mailbox.

About the Author

George Newman was born in Vienna, Austria on August 26, 1936. Two years later, his parents fled the Nazi occupation, taking him to the United States. He grew up and attended public schools in Miami, Florida. After high school graduation, he worked at a variety of jobs ranging from factory helper to printer. Later, after serving three years in the U.S. Coast Guard and receiving an honorable discharge, Newman joined the staff of the *Miami News,* where he worked as a reporter. He later moved to California, where he served on the staffs of the *Redwood City Tribune, Burlingame Advance-Star* and *San Jose Mercury News*, taking time between to earn a Bachelor's degree. He received a Master of Science (psychology) degree from the University of Wisconsin-Milwaukee in 1973. He also served as a part-time faculty member at West Valley College in Saratoga, California from 1973 to 1983.

Among notable achievements, Newman has received the American Political Science Association Award for Distinguished Reporting of Public Affairs; San Francisco Press Club, best news story; South Bay Press Club, best feature story; the Associated Press News Executives Conference, best feature story; and the State Bar of California's Golden Medallion Media Award for outstanding reporting on the administration of justice.

He has served as a volunteer in Big Brothers, a Little League coach and rental housing mediator for the City of Mountain View, California. He also served as a trip leader for the Sierra Club and volunteer tutor for a Soviet refugee program.

Newman now lives in Tucson, Arizona, where he continues to write. His current projects include work on an original screenplay and a couple of book manuscripts. His son, Rick, an actor, resides in Los Angeles.

Share this great book with a friend or family member— you will give great pleasure to all!

101 Ways to be a Long-Distance Super Dad...or Mom Too!
by George Newman

This book is filled with methods that any parent, no matter how far away, can use to spend quality time with their children. A long-distance dad himself, the author wanted to be a part of his son's life after his divorce. As he became more creative about how to accomplish that task, he realized that his experiences would make an extremely valuable guide for others in a similar situation. The suggestions in this book cover a variety of ways in which long-distance parents, grandparents and others can stay in touch.

$9.95   ISBN 1-56875-188-5   Order Number: 188-5

Other educational books from R&E Publishers:

Building Healthy Friendships:
Teaching Friendship Skills to Young People
by Terry A. Beck

Using anecdotes, humor and her unique personal experience, Terry Beck offers a step-by-step approach for helping young people of all ages learn essential friendship skills at home or in the classroom. Parents, educators and the young may use this practical guide in small group settings or on an individual basis to help children learn how to establish healthy relationships throughout their lives. Listening, courtesy, giving, friendliness, loyalty and expectations are among the skills covered.

$9.95   ISBN 1-56875-073-0   Order Number: 073-0

Taking Charge: A Parent and Teacher Guide to Loving Discipline
by Jo Anne Nordling

At last, here is a book that shows both parents and teachers everything they need to know to discipline children effectively and fairly. This easy-to-understand action guide will show you how to handle the most critical disciplinary issues in teaching and raising children. Topics include:

• The four types of misbehavior and what to do about them
• How to encourage positive behavior and discourage negative actions
• How to build self-esteem in children

$14.95   ISBN 1-56875-189-3   Order Number: 189-3

Surviving Summers With Kids:
Fun-filled Activities for All
by Rita B. Herron

It comes every year, the dreaded summer break. When schools close, parents are at the mercy of their unoccupied and restless children. This lighthearted, easy-to-read book is filled with anecdotes and tips for surviving summer vacations with your psyche intact. Written by a teacher and mother.

$9.95   ISBN 1-56875-052-8   Order Number: 052-8

Take Charge Now!
Surviving the Classroom—Tips for Motivating & Inspiring All Teachers
by Rita B. Herron

Finally, the book all teachers have been waiting for! This unique and inspiring book will help to motivate and empower new teachers, as well as delight, encourage and show appreciation for all experienced ones. *Take Charge Now!* is a perfect gift for teachers and a practical guide for students in the field of education.

$9.95   ISBN 1-56875-069-2   Order Number: 069-2

The Winning Feeling:
A Program to Successfully Develop Self-Esteem
by John Kearns & Garry Shulman

Most children idolize athletes and this book teaches them how to apply the winning mindset of champion athletes to the classroom. Teachers and parents can help students of all ages to win in the classroom and in their lives by using the techniques in this powerful new book.

$9.95   ISBN 1-56875-060-9   Order Number: 060-9

How to Start Your Own Successful Day Care:
Run Your Business Properly and Safely
by Alisa Livingstone

This book is for people interested in starting a day care business in their home AND for parents looking for good day care. Licensing, contracts, forms, supplies, safety, nutrition, education and entertainment are covered.

$14.95   ISBN 1-56875-097-8   Order Number: 097-8

ORDER FORM

(May be copied if additional forms are needed)

Please rush me the following books. I want to save money by ordering three books and receiving FREE shipping charges. Orders under three books please include $2.50 shipping. California residents please add 7.75% sales tax.

YOUR ORDER:

Order No.	Title (Please Print)	Qty.	Unit Price	Total Price

Subtotal _____

Sales Tax _____

Shipping _____

101 Ways   **Grand Total** _____

SHIP TO:

Please Print

Name: _____

Organization: _____

Address: _____

City/State/Zip: _____

PAYMENT METHOD:

☐ Check or money order enclosed, payable to R&E Publishers

☐ VISA   ☐ Mastercard   Credit Card Expiration Date: _____

Credit Card No.: ☐☐☐☐ ☐☐☐☐ ☐☐☐☐ ☐☐☐☐

Signature: _____

Telephone: (_____) _____

R&E Publishers, 2132 O'Toole Avenue, San Jose, CA 95131
Tel: (408) 432-3443   Fax: (408) 432-9221